The Fragrance of Sufism

The Fragrance of Sufism

Molana Salaheddin Ali Nader Shah Angha
"Pir Oveyssi"

Shahmaghsoudi (Angha) Heritage Series on Sufism

UNIVERSITY PRESS OF AMERICA, INC.
Lanham   New York   London

University Press of America,® Inc.
4720 Boston Way
Lanham, Maryland 20706

12 Hid's Copse Rd.
Cummor Hill, Oxford OX2 9JJ

ISBN 0-8191-9794-7 (pbk: alk. ppr.)

Cover design, artwork, typography by:
M.T.O. Shahmaghsoudi®

First printing: 1996
Second printing: 1997

Contents

In translating from the Persian, the masculine gender is used in references to God and human being (*"ensan"*). This is partly for convenience but also because the Persian language has no distinct gender denominations; thus, the Persian pronoun *"ou"* may mean "he" as well as "she" with the proper meaning contextually determined.

The
Treasure
on *God's*
Path

Introduction

*T*his book is one of the latest contributions of Hazrat Pir, Molana Salaheddin Ali Nader Shah Angha, to the literature available in English on Sufism. But before introducing the contents of the book to the readers, it is necessary to give some biographical details about the author. The author, it should be emphasized, is a spiritual figure whose intellectual works are shaped and formed by his spiritual lineage and training, as well as his educational background.

Hazrat Pir, Molana Salaheddin Ali Nader Shah Angha, is the forty-second Eminent Pir (Spiritual Leader) of Maktab Tarighat Oveyssi Shahmaghsoudi *(School of Islamic Sufism)* in an unbroken line of succession dating back 1400 years to the time of the Prophet Mohammad (peace be upon him). Born in Tehran, Iran on September 30, 1945, he received the leadership of M.T.O. Shahmaghsoudi from his father on September 4, 1970, when he was only twenty-five.

Hazrat Pir's great-grandfather, Molana Jalaleddin Ali Mir Abolfazl Angha, began the current Renaissance of Sufism, introducing Sufism from a scientific perspective, and became known as the king of the gnostics. In addition to receiving the leadership of the Oveyssi Order, he was given the succession to the Maroufi, Nematollahi, and Zahabieh Orders. The esoteric secrets were entrusted to Hazrat Pir's grandfather, Molana Mir Ghotbeddin Mohammad Angha, who continued the tradition of putting the sublime knowledge of Sufism into scientific language. It is said that if it were not for him, "...the reality of *ma'rifa* (cognition) would never have appeared in our era." His spiritual successor was his son, Molana Shah Maghsoud Sadegh Angha, who was proficient in an amazing number of exoteric and esoteric disciplines, and wrote more than 150 works in prose, as well as in the long standing poetic heritage of Persia. Their ancestry dates back to the seventh Imam of the Shi'a, a direct descendent of the Prophet Mohammad (peace and blessings upon him), as well as to the Safavid Dynasty of Iran.

Surrounded by the spiritual traditions and heritage of Sufism, in the Persian cultural gateway between East and West, Hazrat Pir's training began at birth under the guidance of his grandfather. When he showed signs of special talents, his father began his lengthy and stringent tutelage in the metaphysical sciences. He came to the United States at the age of 16, and continued through college and graduate school, earning degrees in both physics and mathematics. He worked as a mathematics instructor, then as a physicist, while pursuing his metaphysical training. Upon coming back to Iran, he continued his research in the area of physics at the Atomic Energy Commission, until he returned to the United States with his father in 1978.

His father, Molana Shah Maghsoud Sadegh Angha, recognizing his rare spiritual talent, understanding and knowledge, has stated: "Thousands of years are needed to witness such a genius again." Pursuing his father's mission, Hazrat Pir has worked unceasingly to train and educate people from all walks of life and religious backgrounds in the reality of religion. His students include professors, researchers, and scientists in the various fields of the arts, humanities, and sciences. It is Hazrat Pir's conviction that unless each person's inherent goodness, talents, and abilities are excavated, he or she will not know the true meaning of stability, security, freedom, and human dignity. Hazrat Pir emphasizes the need for peace, and has shared his wisdom on attaining personal and global peace in a book by that title.

Hazrat Pir is internationally recognized as the eminent Sufi Master. The global network of centers which he directs serve some 400,000 students. Through his extensive lecture commitments at leading universities in the West, and other scientific and educational institutions, he has presented the depth of the spirituality in Islam, its scientific richness and its relevance for contemporary life. Hazrat Pir has made humanity aware of the invaluable treasure that lies within each person. His mastery of the exoteric and esoteric sciences can be seen in his writings, which reveal the laws of

Existence and the human being's inherent relationship with these laws. He is the author of more than 50 books of poetry and prose focusing on the knowledge embedded in the discipline of Sufism. Only a select few have been translated into English.

This particular work, consisting of three texts — *The Treasure on God's Path, The Approaching Promise,* and *The Secret Word* — is both an introduction to Sufism and a guidebook for the more advanced student. It is a significant work, in that it conveys the essence of Sufism to the modern reader who wishes to inquire and know the reality of the spiritual experience.

Modern men and women are faced daily with existential realities that beg for their attention. However, in many instances, rather than to take the time to reflect on the human condition, they either brush off these mental bleeps on their spiritual screens or dance around them by substituting the futile and fleeting salve offered by drugs for their spiritual exercise. Avoiding responsibility is made possible largely because of the nature of modern society. In a social universe where people are, in the language of William Shakespeare, cabined, cribbed and boxed in their little worlds of anonymity and private suffering, such a state of affairs has come about not because of the lack of spiritual means, but because of the absorbing and crippling nature of our increasingly secular world. Those who are interested in enjoying all the material benefits of our industrial society without necessarily losing their spiritual selves can still do so with sufficient effort. This requires solitude in the full flow of man's spiritual inheritance. Yet, while suggesting this avenue to spiritual self-development, it must be recognized that in the market place of ideas where answers to issues relating to ontology, epistemology, ethics, and eschatology are traded, many contradictory ideas co-exist. Owing to this potential for "babelization" regarding the nature of man and his destiny in the greater scheme of things, the anxious and eager must be warned to tread cautiously in life's spiritual highway.

The book you are about to read is written by someone who is aware of the multiplicity of contending ideas about the human condition. Without apologizing for his position, he spells out the differences between the major contending philosophical schools of thought. He makes it categorically clear that Islam and its teachings on the meaning of life is not only reliable but relevant at all times in the history of humanity. He identifies the Greek and modern schools of Western thought that have dominated the intellectual land-scape of the world for some time now. Within this intellectual tradition, he makes a distinction among those who center existence in the realm of ideas; hence the centrality of ideas in the definition of reality. This view of the world received its greatest and most articulate expression in the writings of Plato. The great Greek philosopher taught his contempo-raries and subsequent generations of thinkers that life on this planet is determined less by material things than by the

Realm of Ideas, for it is in this realm that material reality itself borrows its existence. In the language of Plato, our lives are nothing but false copies of the original idea of humanity in the Realm of Ideas. This conceptualization of the human condition gives rise to a certain attitude towards this world. Those who live by this interpretation of life act and behave in a manner which many who hold alternative views about this spiritual world reject and abhor. Similarly, the rival philosophical materialist position developed by earlier Greek philosophers and improved by Karl Marx and others in the last two centuries, argues for a world where life as we know it is the result of an on-going complex material process. These philosophical materialists tend to deny anything about a Higher Being and for this reason they deny the claims of their fellow humans who embrace the teachings and practices which celebrate the Eternal Creator of the Universe.

Besides these two schools of thought described very well by the author, there are other contemporary schools which are not convinced about the reality of what German philosopher Immanuel Kant called the "Noumenal World." Among these contemporary schools the Positivists have until recently been the most powerful. Deeply rooted in the mainstream of contemporary science, and unwilling to accept any reality that is invisible on their scientific screens, they dismiss off-hand and sometimes arrogantly any articulations of a Transcendental World. It is indeed against this background that we look at the book in your hand.

After having discussed the manner in which the author deals with the contending philosophical schools in the contemporary world, let us now proceed to the discussion of his own ideas about the human condition and the reasons he offers for the claim that Islam is both viable and relevant in our time and at all times. First of all, it should be stated that he conceptualizes man as a being with potentials for spiritual development at four levels. Building on the Qur'anic concept about the three spiritual stages in the evolution of the believer on earth, and taking into account the changing circumstances of the human being, the author tells us that at the lowest level of spiritual development, man is located in the realm of nature where he and all other existential units dance to the music of the Creator's *Kun*.[1]

In the world of nature, the human being can live his or her life in the same manner as the rock, the amoeba and other less complicated life forms. This is the stage of elemental living. At the second level of existence the human being participates in the dynamism of material existence and is sensitive to the interactions between his being-in-itself and the world-in-itself. At the third level the human being is elevated to the point of not only relating to things outside of himself, but the complete material and psychological existence is subject to experience and reflection from within the human being. At the fourth and highest level man is

---

[1]Kun is the Qur'anic word for "Be", that is, whatever God wills comes into being.

focused on himself. He is not only able to tap the spiritual resources locked in the inner recesses of his being, but he is now connected to the Creator because these inner spiritual resources have made it possible for him or her to be pleased with God and himself. Indeed, at this stage in one's spiritual journey, the Qur'anic verse, "To the righteous soul it will be said: 'O Soul, in rest and satisfaction, come back thou to thy Lord, well pleased, and well-pleasing unto Him'" reverberates in the spiritual firmament of the believer. Our author tells us that modern men and women must develop the necessary self discipline to reach the inner resources of their being. Those who have developed these potentials in themselves are no longer slaves and servants of their material world. Rather, their material world is reshaped in accordance with the spiritual demands of their lives.

Following a lengthy discussion of Islamic teachings about the human condition, the author introduces the uninitiated to the complexities and subtleties of the Sufi Way of Life. Building upon the rich legacy of Islam in this area of human spiritual development, and taking into account the realities of modern challenges, the author spells out the various steps and stages to be followed by the seeker of spiritual guidance. But while doing so, he makes it categorically clear to the uninitiated that the traveller on this vast highway needs to follow meticulously the instructions as well as the constant guidance of the Spiritual Guide. In other words, the *salik*, to use a common Sufi term for the student, must always listen to what the Spiritual Guide is saying, for any miscommunication could result in going astray. To prevent taking the wrong exit on this highway, it would help a great deal if the student pays close attention to the words and directions coming from the Spiritual Guide.

This book by a great spiritual leader in the West today deserves our attention. I have read it carefully and found its contents not only a useful guide to the perplexed, to borrow a phrase from a great medieval spiritual teacher, but a well-constructed road map for the modern man and woman interested in finding answers to questions about the meaning of life. It is a book of opportunities and a call to those who have ears to hear.

Sulayman S. Nyang, Ph.D.
April 12, 1995

Professor Sulayman Nyang is a distinguished Professor of African and Islamic Studies at Howard University. He is on the Advisory Council and Adjunct Professor at Georgetown University's Center for Muslim-Christian Understanding. He is the current Vice President of the American Council for the Study of Islamic Societies and a former President of the Association of Muslim Social Scientists. Founding Editor-in-Chief of the *American Journal of Islamic Social Sciences* (AJISS), he is a recognized authority on African, Middle Eastern, and Islamic Affairs. He has published extensively on African affairs and culture, authored and edited *Islam, Christianity and African Identity, Islam: Its Relevance Today,* and *Religious Plurality in Africa.*

He who is sustained

by the hand of God,

Need not fear anyone at all.

Seyr-al Saer va Teyr-al Nader
Molana Shah Maghsoud Sadegh Angha
"Pir Oveyssi"

What exists, in absolute rapture
Glorifies the Essence of Being.

Calligraphy by the hand of
Molana Shah Maghsoud Sadegh Angha

ehold!

How enlightened Father made me,

In His School of Love,

a Pir He made me.

Water was I,

fire He thrust unto my soul,

Of earth was I,

upon the wind He cast me.

Chanteh — Realm of the Sufi
Molana Shah Maghsoud Sadegh Angha
"Pir Oveyssi"

The Treasure on God's Path

بِسْمِ اللهِ الرَّحْمٰنِ الرَّحِيمِ

والحمد لله فسبحان الذى فى قبضة ملكوت
كل شئ وهو القائم الحى القيوم العزيز، كائن
لا عن حدث، موجود لا عن عدم، مع كل شئ لا
بمقارنته وغير كل شئ لا بمزايلة، وضع الملك والملكوت
فسوى منه سبع سموات فيها الشمس والقمر و
النجوم وجعل البروج كل فى فلك يسبحون، وجعل
الليل لمعرفته واليوم مصباحا الرحمة وصلى الله
على رسوله المبعوث المحمود محمد المصطفى وعلى
آله وعترته الطاهرين المعصومين.

In the Name of God
Most Gracious, Most Merciful

*P*raise be to God, the summit of perfection and knowledge who encompasses the divinity of all things. He is the Dominant, the Eternal, the Gracious. He exists, but not by accident, and His existence is not contingent upon anything; He exists, but not from nonexistence. He is with everything, but not in parallel with anything; and He is other than anything but is not separate; He destined the powers and the forces and the heavens, from which He made the seven skies in harmony and balance; within them He placed the sun, the moon, and the stars in their constellations; and everything in the universe, in surrender, forever pulsates to the call of Existence. The night was deemed for knowledge of Him, and the day for the light of His effusions. God's grace be upon His chosen and praised Messenger Mohammad Mostafa and his pure and innocent followers and successors.

In God's Great Name

"The brook, the river, the drop, the sea, and the bubble,
all in one voice say: Water we are, water."

Psalms of Truth
Molana Shah Maghsoud Sadegh Angha
"Pir Oveyssi"

*M*ost people, upon encountering the principles set forth by the *arif* (gnostic), ask with curiosity and uncertainty: What is the message of *irfan* (gnosis) and what lies within the message of the *arif*?

To prepare the necessary framework for communicating words and ideas, and thus laying the foundation for logical understanding and personal experience, requires a lengthy and special preparation on the part of the true and dedicated *salik* (truth seeker) of *irfan*. However, even if in summary form, some of the perplexing aspects of *irfan* may be clarified.

Man's urge to search for and discover new phenomenon, though variously defined by different schools of thought and scientific disciplines, and not limited to any particular time or subject, is, in reality innate to each individual and manifests itself according to each person's capability and aptitude.

The significance of the foregoing proposition lies in man's innate urge to know the reason for his existence, the course of his natural life from its beginning to the present, and to foresee his future, which is undetermined and cannot be foretold by imagination and speculation. This urge, as well as man's genuine need to reach his goals, explains why *irfan* at all levels, times, places, and across all frontiers, has a pervasive and universal appeal. Irrespective of his creed, occupation, class, and opinions, man seeks to explore his capabilities, aptitudes and dimensions. Just as, from the moment of birth, a baby seeks to discover his capabilities by using his sensory and physical abilities and to fulfill his needs and familiarize himself with his environment, so man upon reaching appropriate mental maturity, wishes to know the cause of his existence, his present and future life, and ultimately his death through a vaster sphere. However, those who take this essential need lightly, or ignore it, are trapped and remain beholden to the course of natural events. Those, on the other hand, who use their endowed abilities and natural powers to discover essential truths will find the ultimate answer through devotion and practice of the principles of *irfan*.

Before addressing other topics, we must take up the question of man in his different levels of existence, for he is the center and the cornerstone of all thought, attributes, and actions and, in fact, man is the messenger from the lowest to the highest states of being. It is therefore important for man to know, and ultimately cognize, the foundations and points of his stability, and his relationship with his immediate and wider environment in all its aspects.

Overall, man, in his states of assimilation and congregation, relates and interacts through four different levels that comprise his axis of search, thought, and being:

First, the mysterious inner level, which is the central point of stability of his true character and identity;

Second, the developmental level, which is the locus for the development and interrelationship of the magnetic bodies and for mental, sensory, and psychic powers;

Third, the dependent, indigent, and impressed cellular level, which in fact is the mechanical level of man; and

Fourth, nature, which is the locus for material manifestation and exchange — the laboratory for the examination and experience of man's aptitudes, and the place to satisfy his needs.

Living through any of these four levels gives different experiential and scientific results, each with distinct aspects, characteristics, and dimensions. Proper research for cognizing man is possible only if the level at which man is being researched is recognized, because in each of his levels man is defined and cognized differently. Thus, stability in any of the above four levels designates which aspect of man is the subject of research — from the material to the sublime.

The interrelationship between each of the above-mentioned levels can be distinguished for experimental research, for each of the levels influences and is influenced by the others as they mingle and fuse. For example, nature influences the senses and in turn the senses interpret the events of nature, like audible sound waves emanating from nature. Therefore, each attracting force has a subject of attraction, and the attracted is, in turn, the attracting force.

The empirical and theoretical sciences of mankind, man's scope of thought, and the result of both have direct relationship to which of the above-mentioned levels man finds as his point of stability. That is to say, the empirical scientist, in studying and experimenting with the natural and external environment, namely the physical aspects of nature, wants to know their properties and potential, and ultimately wishes to discover the relevant physical laws so that he may measure, use, and control them for improving the environment for living. The results of his search are, therefore, directed to enhancing the possibilities and potential of man's life by making them harmonious with the laws of nature. The unquestionable scientific advancement of the past few centuries clearly demonstrates the stability of man's powers in the natural levels. At the same time, in reflecting about experimental and theoretical questions, the scientist is also curious about their metaphysical dimension so as to discover and clarify the perplexing issues of life and existence.

The aim of scientific experiments, by individuals or groups, is to know the properties, effects, and dimensions of objects so that, through their control and manipulation, the environment for living may be improved, and ultimately ways and means found to live the present natural life to its end with more tranquility.

The first group, namely the scientists, base their methodology on their intellectual and sensory powers in conjunction with their individual aptitudes, as they manipulate and balance the possibilities of nature to reconstitute new by-products. Hence, this type of knowledge provides the means and a new experiential area for the continuation and improvement of man's natural life, whose results answer mainly the needs of the cellular level of man and a small part of his innate developmental level.

The second group in the history of man may be called the speculative thinkers who have, through reasoning and theoretical speculation, sought to provide logical answers to the definition of man in relation to the congregational environment of his vast world. They are the theologians, the materialistic philosophers, the mathematical scholars, the naturalists, and the sociologists. They define man conceptually as a being or social unit and, placing him before infinite existence, are curious to discover his relationship to the questions of his "being" and "becoming" in existence. Through reason and logic they have related man's "being" to existence. The social theoreticians recognize the "becoming" of man as a social unit according to a set of principles that are in total discord with man's individual, innate state. The conclusions of such groups are derived, and benefit from, the physical environment, their cellular level, and a minor aspect of their inner intellectual and developmental level and sensory powers. It is obvious, then, that this type of research and its resulting speculations and definitions is nothing but reasoning and deduction in words, because its practitioners do not have access to man's central level of stability and identity. This method of induction and deduction, because it is not based on true knowledge, consists of nothing but images and illusions construed in the mind of its advocates in the interplay of the senses and the environment, and explains only a limited aspect, value and dimension of man. Thus with each given variable, different and contradictory results are obtained. For this reason, experimental and analytical psychology and psychotherapy have been unsuccessful. For the same reason most analytical theories and philosophical ideologies have become outdated with later thinkers.

It has been observed that those who execute the principles set forth in social theories often use force, coercion, and influence. Therefore, such general theories do not meet the requirements of man's true identity, since laws must be dominated by man, and not man by laws. This is because thought and the activities of man's sensory level, which are generally a combination of his sensory perceptions, cellular needs, unfulfilled desires, nature and experience, on the one hand, and his cultural heritage, personal and creative aptitudes, on the other, cannot provide the ultimate cognition of the absolute truth of man.

Molana Shah Maghsoud Sadegh Angha[1] in the *Manifestations of Thought* says:

> If a small particle is derailed from its true axis, it will turn the destiny of the whole natural manifestation to an unknown destination, in the sense that the existence of nature as it now is will be altered. These are true yet poetic thoughts which are determined by man's existing sensory perceptions. However, there is a great deal of knowledge enshrined in nature, of which man is unaware. But how can these exact and ordered natural phenomena that follow a precise path of knowledge in the universe be comprehensible to an earthly being like man?

The various extensive levels of man cannot be defined within the scope of his own limited and inadequate comprehension. Just as effective communication between man and his external environment depends on his direct knowledge and domination of the external world, so man's intellectual search for the roots of his inward drives and reactions is a function of his knowledge in relation to his inner world. In this way, harmony is established between the seeker and his inner level, which leads to definite and sound results that otherwise are unobtainable through the study of his outward reactions and appearances.

In view of the foregoing, it is evident that the basis for the research and the results obtained by the thinkers mentioned earlier is limited to the three levels of man which are under the influence of nature and related to it. In the midst of these interactions, man remains a stranger to his inner mysterious level and to his true character and identity. Although the results of such research based on nature indicate a partial discovery of the laws of nature, cognition of the true character and identity of man, which is his authentic and sublime aspect, remains unknown. Thus, cognition of man's reality is other than analysis of the organism, its natural needs, and the exterior forces influencing it. This is a basic point for the thoughtful individual who asks: Who is man? He who is wrapped with such complexity within the different levels is the subject of which branch of science? How may one know him?

The history of thought turns man's attention to the third group, and we are faced with the following question: What message and results do the Prophets bring to man?

If one looks sincerely and in an unbiased manner at the teachings of the Prophets and the results of their research, it will be seen that their message invites man to an unchanging reality in which time and space cannot interfere, that is to say to absolute knowledge, cognition and true research, a reality in which man may cognize the truth. Cognition of man's truth is the essence of the message of the Prophets, which is the way of release from the confines of nature and the means for the cognition of man's true character and identity, which is the gateway to the cognition of another mysterious level of man.

The words and the message of true men are not audible to those entrapped by nature, for the latter are deaf to the message. In other words, an individual who is confined within the limits of nature, whose knowledge and actions are immured within it, has no chance to become acquainted with the true words. Therefore, words such as God, paradise, hell, requital, charity, self, soul, Eternal Tablet, angel, death, and many other truths have no awakening response in his mental constitution. And whenever such words are propounded in the society of men, they are considered in a physical context, rendered and practiced in accordance with men's own wishes, defined by and endowed with rituals, and given myriad other connotations based on ignorance and prejudice. What is evident from the words and inner meaning of the message of the Prophets is that they invite man to *irfan* — cognition of the true realms — so that he may experience the inherent truth of existence through his own true level. As the Holy Prophet of Islam, Hazrat Mohammad (peace and blessings upon him) has said, "Whosoever cognizes his true self has cognized God." This is the true declaration of human rights for research and attainment of the reality of man, which is other than ideas and thoughts generally constructed by changing and influential nature. Therefore, it is now clear why the declarations and laws promulgated by the true personalities, that is the Prophets, do not appeal to those involved at the level of nature. Man, in abiding by inherited and outdated ideas and beliefs devoid of the truth of life, is like a thirsty person who takes a desert mirage for water.

The foregoing introduction brings us to the topic at hand, which is *irfan* and *soluk* (journey on the Path).

1. Irfan

The word *irfan* generally means cognition, familiarization and acquaintance, and for the *arif* it is the way to cognize the attributes and essence of God through the discovery of the heavenly kingdom and secrets of man's heart through vision and revelation.

The word cognition has also been used by the philosophers. However, there is a great difference between the method of the *arif* and that of the philosopher regarding the attainment of true cognition. The *arif* cognizes the truth through certainty, heart-visions, and stability in the reality of identity of his true personality. But, for the philosopher, the method of cognition is based upon reasoning, analogy, and logic, deduced from the mental faculties, from sensory inputs, and from observation of natural phenomena.

Man's approach in general, and the philosopher's in particular, can be classified into two categories. The first group believes that cognizing reality is beyond man's capacity and is therefore impossible; the Skeptic and Sophist Schools are in this category. The second is of the opinion that cognizing the truth is possible only by logical reasoning or self-discipline and purification. The Peripatetics, Deductionists, Platonists, and neo-Platonists belong to this group.

To summarize their ideas and way of thinking we can say: The Peripatetic, Aristotle being its renowned proponent, believes that cognizing reality and truth is possible only through reasoning, and matters that are proven by logical reasoning are truths even though they are not accepted by religious laws. The Deductionist says that though cognizing and acquainting reality is possible only through logical reasoning, only those truths that are approved by religious laws are acceptable.

The Platonist and neo-Platonist do not consider the mind as the ultimate means for experience and understanding because they assert that it is a function of the sensory faculties. They maintain that comprehension and mental perception are in a constant state of change. Thus all views and results deduced from them are subject to change. Therefore, the cognition of truth is possible only when transitory inclinations and natural qualities do not influence the reality of man. This important task is achieved only through self-discipline and purification, in which case there is no need to become involved in the method of reasoning. By self-discipline and purification, one can cognize the truth through one's heart. Therefore, according to the Platonist, this is the right way and the one and only elevated truth, whether or not it is accepted by religious laws.

The *arif's* method regarding cognition of truth is through self-discipline, purification, concentration, and heart-meditation. But only those inward discoveries which are approved and emphasized by religious laws are the true ones; otherwise he considers them as visual and auditory deviations, in other words, it is being misled by the senses.

The above classification is according to the views expressed and passed on by previous philosophers. Since they have not given any definite or indisputable method to their ideas, the results derived from their ideas invite such classification. In my opinion, it is also possible to classify the proponents of philosophic ideas as: philosophers, theologians, naturalists, and metaphysicians.

The approach of these four groups to attaining cognition is based on logical reasoning, the mind, or solely self-discipline and mathematical theories; the method of cognition in *irfan* is totally different.

Sheikh Razi,[2] the author of *Mirsad-ol Ibad,* has divided the subject of cognition into three major types. He believes that cognition can be achieved by speculation, theoretical observation, and heart-vision. Regarding the speculative way of cognition he has said: "The common people follow the theoretical view, among them are unbelievers, Moslems, Jews, Christians, Zoroastrians, heretics, philosophers, naturalists, and materialists. And they all share one common point, which is sensory perception. There is no salvation through such an approach except for those whose mental deductions are confirmed by the light of faith. Thus, they can attest and rise to the edict of faith, for the nature of the seed of the soul will only produce the fruit of faith."

Molana Shah Maghsoud Sadegh Angha, Pir Oveyssi, says:

> Man, in his own truth, can perceive a perfect specimen of everything which is found in the universe. What causes man to be degraded from his eminent position is his dependence and reliance on his perceptions which are distorted by the senses in proportion to their capabilities. If the self of man would be refined, he would be elevated to his utmost spiritual state which would surpass natural causes. He, then, would attain the state of Man. He, in this case, is the meaning of the name of God and true worship. Therefore, his identity is honored with the Viceregency of God in nature.[3]

Shabestari's *Golshan-e Raz,*[4] Rumi's *Masnavi,*[5] Attar's *Mossibat Nameh,*[6] and many other works which explain *irfan,* contain precise points of inward revelations that cannot be considered as individual opinions and illusions.

However, from the philosopher's point of view, the matter of cognition is attainable in two ways. First, cognition is obtained through reasoning, debate, and investigation of objects regarding their matter, essence, time, space and properties. For example, the concept of cause and effect is so deeply imprinted in the minds of such philosophers that they evaluate all universal truths by it. Farabi[7] in his book *Fusus-ol Hikam*, referring to this type of reasoning says: "If the being's existence be without Existence, it is necessary that the being himself be the cause of his own existence; therefore, it must be said that if an object is the cause of its own existence, it is null and void."

Second, the Naturalists want to prove the absolute essence through movement, and the cause of movement, therefore, classifying movement into the carnal and the divine. According to their interpretation movement is change and motion from one place to another. Thus they ignore the absolute essence of movement because for them changes and alterations are manifested only through their effects. The truth of movement cannot be discovered in this manner because only the sequential and spatial manifestations of movement are considered.

These scientists have also classified the "selves" into the vegetative, the animal, and the human selves, designating them as appearances. Regarding the appearance of the human form they have based their theory on the cause, which is known as essence and, unavoidably, they have separated it from the world of matter. This type of reasoning, even though correct on the basis of their theories, keeps the truth of essence so far out of reach that no aspect of cognition is contained in it.

The Metaphysicians, in turn, have considered the subject of appearances and say that the universe has been created because of necessity, that each manifestation or appearance needs a creator and, therefore, the creator must be the Absolute Essence.

I have to emphasize that, considering all the above, man in his thoughts posits the creation of his own mind in the place of receiving and cognizing the truth. In other words, he takes illusion and imagination for truth.

The *arif* says: What exists and is constant, is truth. The philosophers search for the truth in the changeable; thus their views have no constancy nor stability, and they are not disposed to the reception of truth.

The *arif* attains his goal through reliance and ascent, which is the way of the guiding Imams (heavenly teachers), and with certainty journey's to the summit of cognition. He attests to: "As also in your own selves: will you not then see" *(Holy Qur'an, 51:21)*? Meanwhile, the philosopher is adrift in analyses of introductory definitions, theoretical assumptions, and examinations of nature and its manifestations.

Through the essence of love and the guidance of the radiant pure soul of the *Pir* (Spiritual Teacher), the *arif* has cognized the path. God knows his secret and he has reached the state of annihilation in truth: "All individuality will perish and the Face of thy Lord will abide for ever — Full of Majesty, bounty and honor" *(Holy Qur'an, 55:26,27)*. But the philosopher, depending on the support of his inconstant mind and unfounded theories, is proud and arrogant of that which he has not: "If not Him, you worship nothing but names which you have named, — you and your fathers — for you are not guided by a heavenly Teacher: God is the source and none else" *(Holy Qur'an, 12:40)*.

2. Oneness of Existence (Monism)

One of the prevalent theories propounded, researched, and pondered upon by thinkers is the Oneness of Existence. Some philosophers, because of their failure to grasp the subject, have either rejected the Oneness of Existence or, in expressing their opinions, have tried to cover the subject with a multitude of explanations and definitions, or have denied it totally. The propagation of views regarding the self-existent and the possible, existence and being, the physical world and metaphysical, and their efforts to show the various states and different aspects of them has created the idea of dualism, and each group has developed its own followers and its own approach to research and the propagation of ideas. It is necessary to point out that, when research is conducted in isolation by different thinkers, the results are generally unfavorable because the discovery of the reality of existence and objects is possible only when, both theoretically and experimentally, no aspect remains unknown. In other words, the researcher should be in a position to know the subject so completely that he knows all its aspects — the outer as well as the inner aspects. Therefore, the knowledge gained by man through sensory inputs to the mind will not lead to the discovery and cognition of truth. Cognition and true knowledge depend solely on the Infinite Identity. The *arif* cognizes and the philosopher investigates to know.

The *arif* believes in the Oneness of Existence. In his innermost "book" is unlimited Existence; there is none other but He, and He is Absolute. Thus, all possibilities and qualities, all attributes and states, and all conditions manifested before man are bestowed by His boundless grace and His Essence. This is not in the sense of separation or duality between Him and man, but of the Oneness of Existence incarnate in man in the full horizon of his awareness. He is not in things, He is unquantifiable. Appearances are the reflections of Truth, and the Truth is the source of all manifestations. He is the essence of goodness and beauty, the summit of perfection and grace. What exists cannot be other than it is, and absolute cognition for man is beholding the Absolute Truth in the Journey of "self" to "I."

Therefore, *irfan* considers energy as the reality of matter but, in the limited sensory world, does not take the different aspects of energy as the ultimate goal or purpose of the natural life. The ultimate case for the Oneness of Existence is the manifestation of the being, just as life and its inexorable continuation cannot be denied in manifestations, and life in an insular form is not possible. "To God belong the East and the West: Whichever way you turn, there is the Presence of God. For God is All-Pervading, All-Knowing" (*Holy Qur'an, 2:115*).

In explaining the Oneness of Existence, the *arif* believes that objects are reflected images in the mirrors of Existence, and gives the following example: If you place mirrors of different shapes and sizes — large and small; convex, concave, and other shapes — in your six spatial directions, and place a luminous object or a being in the center, the reflection of the luminous object or a being will have an infinite number of images in these mirrors which, in fact, are the reflections of the countless dimensions of a single entity. Investigating the different shapes and reflections originating in the truth will not solve man's problem; on the contrary, the truth of reflections is in the reality of their centrality. The true reality of any object lies in the core of its existence. Therefore, those who investigate the various images and shapes reflected in the mirrors discover only the reflected images and different qualities and have no knowledge concerning the truth itself. The clear result in this example is that the reflections of the Eternal Reality are numerous and Oneness is the Eternal Truth.

> Beginning and end are but our own creation,
> For Truth has neither beginning nor end,
> Even though seen in myriad manifestations.

> The atom, the sun, the galaxies, and the universe,
> Are surely but names, images, and forms.
> One they are in reality, and only one.[8]

The invitation to such unity is everlasting and, in fact, Existence calls His children to the Truth. The images produced by the senses and the intervening reflections of sensory perceptions create figures in the mind, and in the physical dimension appearances and events are barriers to the discovery of Oneness. As the Holy Prophet Mohammad (peace and blessings to him) has said explicitly on this point: "The physical world is the prison of the believer."[9]

The Oneness of Existence in the sanctuary of the *arif's* heart has no duality nor heresy, knows no boundaries, and is colorless; it is not from Nonexistence, for Nonexistence is not, and Existence is unique.

The vastness of beings, the infinite nature, the expanse of dimensions, the fields of forces, and the infinite universe are a unified system in which dispersion, emptiness, togetherness, transmigration and reincarnation, imperfection, and perfection have no part.

> All is all, together or alone,
> All by all, silently hum the call.[10]

Such a unity has neither beginning nor end, for it is timeless, and there is no place for Him to be known by location or attributes. He is everything but He is not a thing. All manifestations are the single melody of His symphony. He is absolute freedom that knows not and accepts no attachments, and is not bound to any restrictions and is subject to no limitations.

> Countless stages and appearances existence holds,
> Just as water upon which bubbles form.
> What is the bubble but water?[11]

The Master of the enlightened, Hazrat Hossein-ibn Ali[12] (peace be upon him), has said: "O God, there is no creation unless it is the manifestation of You, the Almighty." The explanation of such Oneness in the words of the Holy Saints of God and the eminent *arif* is testament to their cognition of the infinite Existence.

Man's balanced centrality of heart, purified from redundancies, can cognize and attest to the Oneness of Existence, for which the Absolute can only cognize the Absolute. Mola-al-Movaheddin Ali (peace be upon him) has said: "All comes from Him, and He guides all things and He is the Omniscient. He is Allah, the Eternal."[13]

Molana Mir Ghotbeddin Mohammad Angha, Pir Oveyssi has said: "No one can imagine the beginning, the end, and the intermediate points of infinity, because all of its points are endowed with all attributes, and the essence of abundance pervades all. How can you touch Him, when He is everywhere? How can you journey towards Him, when He is everywhere? Cognizing Him is only possible through your complete annihilation, which gives you a vital awareness. O, my God, increase my ecstasy in Thee!"[14]

3. Seyr-va-Solouk - The Horizons of Awareness

The direct bridge to the absolute Truth is the reality of a pure and dedicated *salik* whose real seeking comes from Him. Therefore, he wishes to know and discover Eternity which is the closest point. Hence, the salek is the chosen of God. Therefore, as soon as the seed of godly prosperity is planted in the heart of the *salik*, by divine confirmation he is entrusted to the inwardly revealed *Pir*. This is the real meaning of the blessings of God. In this case by way of His Guardianship, all thoughts, selfishness, pride, and the untamed mind of the *salik* are led from the state of agitation and decline to the path of virtue, and the *salik* reaches his awareness. Through such discipline the *salik* diligently undergoes treatment, as a patient under the care of a physician. You cannot give all your life and assurance to anyone, for no one can be trusted for the unknown path. Hence, for the assurance of the heart, the *Pir* must be inwardly cognized in the heavens by the *salik*, and his teachings shall be practiced outwardly and inwardly, sincerely and faithfully. The heavens are the horizons of awareness and the earth is the domain of oblivion. Can the one in slumber awaken the sleeper?

In fact, cognition of the heavenly reality of the *Pir* and a burning love are both the way and the goal for the *salik*. So guided, the devout *salik* refrains from all redundancies, superficial and unnecessary attachments, and truthfully turns his face and all concerns to the one and only Truth.

One of the major principles of *irfan* is that man never attains knowledge of something which he does not have within himself. This means that the perceiver and the perceived must have an intuitive harmony of existence, so that the ability of cognition may be accomplished. To stabilize in such a reality, the *salik* endeavors continually to forego sleep and illusions, until such time that he is endowed with the attributes of He, the Ever Alive, the Omnipresent, and to be unique in the attainment of godliness which is his maxim.

> Do you think you are a microcosm? Embodied in you
> is the macrocosm.[15]

The Great Master, my father, Molana Shah Maghsoud Sadegh Angha, has stated in his book *The Hidden Angles of Life*:

> If the most elevated and Perfect Man, whose being in
> existence is not extraneous, hears not His voice
> inwardly and knows Him not, what other way is left
> for the cognition of God?

Love for attaining the truth of God makes the *salik* who seeks guidance only from his *Pir*, truly devout and generous. His actions are in devotion and purity; in calamities he is patient, and the pain of separation he endures in the hope of reunion. He stands firm against all indulgence and wastefulness and does not rely on delusions and uncertainty. In confronting the rebellious natural self with the grace of the *Pir*, he is courageous and unswerving. With total inward humility and reverence he fully submits to the guidance of the *Pir* who guards him against all perils, and he in no way disobeys or strays from the commandments of his *Pir*. In this way he can begin his journey with purity and truth: "Whoever seeks me, receives me, and whoever seeks me, knows that I am the gate."[16]

> Seeking the truth of God is not through the limited mind,
> The Pir is the only guide,
> His guidance cannot be interpreted nor judged.
>
> Do not step on the path to God without a guide,
> For the wing of Gabriel was burnt on this path,
> From the fire Divine.[17]

Thus, the *salik* in the Maktab Tarighat Oveyssi Shahmaghsoudi will discover the horizons of awareness without interruption and hesitation under the guidance of the *Pir.* These are:

Zikr *(to remember)* — Remembering God at all times: "Do remember Me, and I am remembering you."[18]

Fikr *(to think, meditate)* — Persisting on the truth of meditation to attain the state of annihilation.

Sahar *(to awaken)* — Awakening of soul and body through the teachings of the *Pir.*

Jui'i *(to hunger)* — Anxiously eager to receive the truth, and keeping the heart and mind constantly ready for the disclosure of the secrets of the heart and revelations.

Suamt   *(to observe silence)* — Ceasing to think and talk about worthless things, purification of the heart from desires.

Saum   *(to fast)* — Fasting of body, mind and heart; refraining from involvement in exterior delusions and imagination; and inwardly abstaining from desires, wishes, and duality.

Khalvat   *(to observe solitude)* — Praying in solitude, externally and internally, being free of all attachments and impurities.

Khidmat   *(to serve)* — Dissolving in the truth of the *Pir* and finally dissolving in the truth of Existence, God.

To reach the point where the seeker sees nothing but God, there are seven stages in which the *salik* must be stabilized and balanced:

The state of natural strength and pleasure — natural strength and pleasure refer to eating, drinking, sleeping, and so on. The *salik* must pass this stage, be content and moderate in his natural appetites, for he must separate his identity from those of animals and plants.

The state of self — through this stage the *salik* should sever all dependence and start a quiet and solitary life. He must begin with the prayers, obey religious laws and, through repentance and endeavor, reach the point where he can step outside his illusive and imaginary world.

The state of heart — the word "heart" is used here to highlight the firm level through which man is elevated from the inferior stages. The heart is the gateway to the hidden world of the truthful *salik*.

The state of soul — the heart is the connection between soul and self. The *salik* in this state, is free from earthly attachments and sentiments, and enters the realm of spirituality.

The state of secret — here the *salik* cognizes the Truth and thenceforth everywhere he looks he sees nothing but God.

> From the particle to the sun, all are manifest by God,
> From the seen and unseen, there is none but God.[19]

The state of hidden — the *salik* at this stage, sees and hears nothing but God. He is dissolved in God: the *salik* and the sought are one. In this state there is no ignorance at all and the truth of life is revealed.

> Such knowledge is for those who know God,
> Thus, there is no god but God.[20]

The state of more hidden — through this stage where the *salik* has ended the circle of eternity, he is no longer aware of his annihilation. This is the stage for the Kingdom of the Supreme Being, as God has said:

> Behold, thy Lord said to the angels: 'I will designate the Viceregent on earth'.[21] Everything will perish, except His own Face.[22]

This is the state of perfection in *seyr-va-soluk,* where the earth and the sky cannot be contained therein, as the Holy Prophet Mohammad (peace and blessings to him) has said:

> The earth and sky cannot contain me but the heart of my devout believer is my dwelling.[23]

The most genuine and supreme goal of existence is the creation of the truth of man in this stage. He is freed from all deceptive explanations, perceptions, definitions, and natural constraints, and is led to the fount of *irfan,* and thus to absolute freedom, tranquility, and eternal existence. For this reason it has been said: "A Sufi is ashamed in both worlds,"[24] which means that he sees and desires none other but God, for he has nothing to present in either world.

> He who ever a trace of awareness of himself has,
> Is not in the least aware of God.

Molana Shah Maghsoud Sadegh Angha in *Chanteh — Realm of the Sufi,*[25] has said:

> Until there remains your self with you,
> Only yourself do you worship,

From the cup of ignorance your drunkenness comes,
Nothing are you, and less than nothing
Until you are you,
Do you know who you are?
When from self you are freed,
You are all.

Man, pure in heart, listened to the inner call of Truth, and heard the Magnificence of the Almighty God and witnessed His divine Presence, and so loved Him. The sign of affection of lovers is that they leave everything from both worlds and keep the bond of the Beloved; this is the great secret of existence.

Leyla's tale of love in words cannot be told, If not within Majnun, then in whom can it be known?[26]

God only must be worshipped. His blessings, His grace, and His mercy be upon Mohammad (peace and blessings to him) and his holy descendants.

Salaheddin Ali Nader Shah Angha
26th Aban 1363
23rd Safar 1405
17th November 1984

Glossary

Arif — (*arif bi'llah*, knowing God) one who has attained *irfan*, i.e., gnostic cognition of the union with God, commonly equated with a Sufi.

Irfan — gnostic cognition of the all-pervasiveness of God, the highest attainment of the Sufi experience.

Imam — divinely inspired leader or teacher, in the Shi'a tradition one of a sequence of persons carrying the divine spark and hence infallible in the matters of teaching and doctrine.

Ka'ba — (the central shrine of Islam in Mecca) in Sufi usage it means the "altar of the heart".

Khezr — in the Qur'an called al-Khadir, the guide of the Prophet Moses (*Holy Qur'an, 18:65-82*). In Sufi literature, *Khezr* is the Spritual Teacher who guides the *salik* to union with God.

Leyla & Majnun — name of two lovers in a famous legend by that name. They are the archetypal lovers in Arabic and Persian literature, who were separated from each other and died from grief of separation. Majnoun's love for Leyla is symbolic of the soul's longing for unification with God.

Pir — in Persian, the traditional title of the head of a Sufi order (*tarighat*) endowed with the highest authority for the teaching and transmission of gnostic insight.

Salik — seeker of truth, one who proceeds on the path toward *irfan* under the guidance of a Spritual Teacher.

Seyr — spiritual journey of the *salik*.

Soluk — the stages of gradual purification the *salik* passes toward attainment of *irfan*.

Vali — (ar. 'friend, intimate') in Sufi usage a saint, a man close to God.

Endnotes

1. Angha, Molana Shah Maghsoud Sadegh: The forty-first Holy Teacher of M.T.O. Shahmaghsoudi. Revered by scholars, scientists, students and devotees as the symbol of knowledge, wisdom, eloquence, compassion and love. His numerous writings (over 150 works) in the sciences, literature, philosophy, and religion have brought the sublime discipline of *irfan* within the reach of those seeking the true meaning of life, bridging the unnecessary separation which has existed between physics and metaphysics since antiquity.

2. Razi, Sheikh Najmeddin: 13th century Persian Sufi poet from Hamadan. One of the twelve disciples of Sheikh Majdeddin Baghdadi, who was one of the disciples of Sheikh Najmeddin Kobra, the sixteenth Holy Teacher of M.T.O. Shahmaghsoudi. Sheikh Razi was a contemporary of Jalaleddin Rumi whom he met in Turkey. In addition to *Mirsad ol Ibad*, he has several other outstanding works; among them are: *Bahr ol-Haqa'iq wa-I-na'ani* (Ocean of Realities and Meanings, an explication on *The Holy Qur'an*), and *Ishq wa Aghl (Love and Reason)*.

3. Angha, Molana Shah Maghsoud Sadegh: *Manifestations of Thought*, Lanham, MD: University Press of America, 1988.

4. Shabestari, Sheikh Mahmoud: 13/14th century Persian Sufi who died at the age of thirty three, having attained the highest state of spiritual realization. He wrote *Golshan-e Raz* (The Secret Garden), in which he speaks of the Perfect Man, the stages of development and spiritual realization, and reveals the truth about the knowledge within each atom.

5. Rumi, Molana Jalaleddin Molavi Balkhi: Moslem saint, mystic and poet of the 13th century. Rumi was raised in a religious family. He met Sheikh Attar in Neishapour, who gave him *The Book of Secrets*, a mystical treatise which influenced Rumi from an early age. Rumi is one of the best-known Sufis in the West. Professor R.A. Nicholson, who spent a life-time studying the works of Rumi, writes: "Jalaleddin found in the stranger that perfect image of the Divine Beloved which he had long been seeking. He took him away to his house, and for a year or two they remained inseparable. Sultan Valad likens his father's all-absorbing

communion with this 'hidden saint' to the celebrated journey of Moses in company with Khadir (*Qur'an*, XVIII 68-80), the Sage whom Sufis regard as the supreme hierophant and guide of travelers on the Way to God."

6. Attar, Sheikh Farideddin: 12th/13th century Persian Sufi, born in Neishapour. Attar was educated at the theological school attached to the shrine of Imam Reza (peace be upon him), the eighth Holy Imam of the Shi'a in Mashhad. He travelled extensively and finally settled in Neishapour where he became a druggist and wrote poetry. His search for the Divine culminated in his celebrated work *The Conference of the Birds*. He is also the author of *Tadheirat-al Awliya*, a biographical presentation of Moslem saints and mystics.

7. Al-Farabi, Abu-Nasr: 10th century Moslem philosopher who was born into a Turkish military family and studied in Baghdad. He established the classical tradition of the Moslem philosophers, leaning towards the social and political analysis of Islam.

8. Angha, Molana Shah Maghsoud Sadegh: *Chanteh — Realm of the Sufi*. Verdugo City, CA: M.T.O. Shahmaghsoudi Publications, 1988.

9. Nahj-ol Fasahah: *The recorded teachings of the Holy Prophet of Islam*, translated by Abolghassem Payandeh. Tehran: Sazman Entesharat Javidan, Mohammad (the Holy Prophet of Islam). *Nahj-ol Fessaheh* (13th Ed.). Tehran: Sazman Entesharat Javidan, 1980.

10. Angha, Molana Shah Maghsoud Sadegh: *The Epic of Existence*. Verdugo City, CA: M.T.O. Shahmaghsoudi Publications, 1986.

11. Angha, Molana Shah Maghsoud Sadegh: *Chanteh — Realm of the Sufi*. Verdugo City, CA: M.T.O. Shahmaghsoudi Publications, 1988.

12. Imam Hosein ibn Ali [626-680 A.D.]: third Holy Imam of the Shi'a, younger son of Imam Ali and Hazrat Fatemeh — daughter of the Holy Prophet of Islam — (peace and blessings be upon them). He lived most of his life in Medina under the surveillance of the Caliph. Refusing to pledge allegiance to the Umayyed caliph Yazid, he deemed it necessary to go into battle against Yazid as protest against the injustice inflicted in the name of Islam. He and his followers were massacred at Karbala.

13. Ali ibn Abi Taleb (Amir-al Mo'menin). *Nahj-ol Balaghah (The Teachings of Amir-al Mo'menin Ali)*: translated by Haj Seyd Ali Naghi Feyz-ol-Islam. Tehran: Entesharat Faghih, 1985. Amir-al Mo'menin Ali (peace be upon him) is the first Holy Imam of the Shi'a [600-661 A.D.]. He was brought up under the care and affection of the Holy Prophet of Islam. He is the first man, and second person to have accepted Islam at the hands of the Prophet. At all times he accompanied the Prophet to help and protect him from his enemies. He recorded the verses of the *Holy Qur'an* and discussed them with the Prophet as soon as they were revealed. He devoted all his life to the service of God for the welfare of humanity. He is known as the personification of love, justice, wisdom, courage, humbleness, kindness, generosity, eloquence, and knowledge.

14. Angha, Molana al-Moazam Hazrat Mir Ghotbeddin Mohammad: *From Fetus to Paradise — The Evolutionary States of Man.* He is the fortieth Holy Teacher of M.T.O. Shahmaghsoudi. It has been said: "If it were not for our Lord Mohammad, son of Mir Abolfazl Angha, the reality of *irfan* and knowledge would never have appeared in our era." He is the author of numerous books in prose and verse on *irfan*, the sciences, and the humanities.

15. *Nahj-ol Balaghah.*

16. Ibid.

17. Angha, S.M.S.: *Chanteh—Realm of the Sufi.*

18. *The Holy Qur'an*, 2:153.

19. Angha, S.M.S.: *The Epic of Existence.*

20. Ibid.

21. *The Holy Qur'an*, 2:30.

22. *The Holy Qur'an*, 28:88.

23. *Nahj-ol Fasahah.*

24. Angha, Molana Shah Maghsoud Sadegh Angha: *Al-Rasa'el.* Lanham, MD: University Press of America, 1986.

25. Angha, S.M.S.: *Chanteh — Realm of the Sufi.*

26. Angha, Molana Shah Maghsoud Sadegh: *Shahed va Mashhoud* and *Seyr-al Saer va Teyr-al Nader.* San Francisco: IKM Printing, 1983.

The
Approaching
Promise

Introduction

*I*n reading *The Approaching Promise* by Molana Salahed-din Ali Nader Shah Angha, the forty-second *Pir* (Spiritual Master) of the Maktab Tarighat Oveyssi Shahmaghsoudi, we are aware of the eminence of its author. The poem is a vessel of spiritual and religious thought for which I have not been formally prepared; yet it is that of a poet as well as a prophet, and so something can belong to all of us who live by a love and interest in language. We are invited in. Poetry is the property of those who can realize it, and it is in this light that we approach the words of a distinguished Sufi Master. Poetic thought shows us the mind and soul of the seer . . . Poetic language reveals the hand of the sayer. With this entitlement we enter the text to experience the force field of the writer's reality in hopes of describing what is found.

The preamble to *The Approaching Promise* holds the statement that its four elements are written in terms of "the axis of Four, Five, Seven, Nine, and Six." We are told that the document was a revelation to Hazrat Pir. For those of us who have followed his recent literature, we are familiar with his work as divine revelation and its subsequent commitment to the page. The fact that *The Approaching Promise* flows in lines of specific length and number is perhaps not necessary knowledge for the reader, but it is of more than slight interest to the writers among us. Those of us who try to harness the moving word will marvel at lines that fall into specific mathematical patterns. To attempt such symmetry and to consciously arrange it is beyond that which most writers can accomplish or are willing to do. Relative to this text, then, is the mystery in its arrangement of words and lines that assume a natural mathematical unity, and finally we accept this more as inspirational than craft.

The text is a blueprint in which the forces-water, wind, earth, fire — are our guides. Each section can be described as a prayer, a chant, a prophesy. There is an infinite question posed after each section. The questions asked by Hazrat Pir are simply, "What happened to That? What became of It?" This reiteration occurs at the end of each of the four sections. By posing these questions Hazrat Pir asks us to evaluate what we have, what we have lost, what we have not used, what we have foregone. He brings us this message — our given treasure — with subtle, penetrating kindness. We notice in the first reading that each of the four stanzas are in eleven lines, and each begins with the word That. Through the use of fire, wind, water, and earth, the writer speaks to us of the journey of light — our existence beyond the elements of fire, wind, water and earth which are the basis for the physical forms of beings.

In his words, Hazrat Pir gives us the sun of knowledge. He describes it as "a radiant magnificent star . . . that descends and penetrates." Through his eyes, we perceive particles of light drifting from the dust of the heavens. A brilliance of thought is inflamed by such dramatic phrases as "feverish hearts," "breath of life," "frenzy of love," "shooting star." These phrases also create a motion within the stanza. The first stanza, then, sets the tone for the whole. Its content creates the crystal of the poet's seeing: a mirror connecting all life and experience . . . moving, moving through eternity like a star "descending and penetrating." In the subsequent lines of the first three stanzas we are given a listing of the exquisiteness of our existence — "that lustrous gleaming pearl," "that water drop," "the fields of endearing madness," "that entrusted jewel" — which we come to know is our essence and the heart's crystal we are born to carry. We are told of our perfection . . . the promise of perfection . . . and how we can be alive with its lustre. It is a poet we read. Hazrat Pir's words bring us close into the radiance of vision. We can understand interpretively the truth seen through his eyes. There is no way we can imagine the exact transference from the Persian language, but the imagery in this translation speaks for the probable beauty of the original.

The fourth section describes how we have castigated our gift. The words now are strong: dust, carcass, cesspool, mud. The language is stark in contrast to the previous stanzas that shimmer with the flowers and fruit of the poet's mind. The song turns harsh as children of the earth are described as "children of greed." The dust of the heavens descends to become "a swampland," and we are among those destined to die with our secret unrealized: "How can I not divulge, this was the treasure that was interred." The living treasure described by the poet dies with us. The poet's final cry is movement back from pain to freedom, however resigned: "Though I am enclosed in the coercion of time, yet the resplendent flame of this lantern I am." So ends the text.

The writing moves from an unenclosed, unlimited gift of glory through a bitter prophesy, leaving us with questions. Earthly confusions make us mistake our clumsy motions for flight. The message throughout is of the danger of such confusion. Will we die of spiritual hunger craving the illusion of food? It points out that the nourishment is in all time within us. But "What happened to That" — the work points again to our potential wreckage. The poem speaks of this world with a voice some of us may not hear. But through the poetry of its cry, the reader can appreciate and understand the promise of liberation and the dangers of captivity. Caught within the strivings of the world, we are told not to mistake activity for spiritual motion. The poem's structure is in five parts. It gains momentum through its listings and phraseology, and most especially through the repetition of a single word framing each line. It asks, at the end of each stanza of eleven lines, Where did all this go? The song ascends in three parts, becomes a dissonant cry in part four, and resolves itself back to song and a personal plea at its ending.

What is there for us to carry away from this small document? For the reader, there is a canon of thought, which is visually extraordinary, as well as an understanding of poetry and its cultural sources. There is — for those interested in the method by which experience is converted to poetry — the ecstasy of the singer and the enchantment of the song. In the poem's content there is a warning of quicksand and the choice given for immortality. This poem is a small symphony to all the senses. As modern individuals, if we take one message from its content, it may be a simple one — that unenlightened worldly activity will lose the soul. This prayer in five parts streams toward silence and takes us with it toward wonder. For those of us receptive to the visionary poem, it is a box of jewels. For those who wish serenity through poetry, reading it may be a beginning.

Grace Cavalieri
September 30, 1988
Washington, D.C.

Grace Cavalieri is a teacher and poet. She is the author of five books of poetry and eighteen plays, which have been produced throughout the country for stage and radio. Her career covers almost every aspect of teaching writing and broadcasting. After setting up a writing program for Antioch College, she became associate director in programming for the Public Broadcasting Service. She was senior program officer in media for the National Endowment for the Humanities and is host/producer of the only ongoing poetry program in the nation now in its twelfth year of broadcast. "The Poet and the Poem" is produced on WPFW-FM in Washington, D.C., and is distributed nationally to public radio stations.

The Approaching Promise

He, The Exalted Lord God

Through intricate labyrinths revolves the way
to the hidden secrets of heart.

And within His hand lies the key to this
treasure's door.

Should the hand of Him, the treasure's Lord,
open your treasure's door,

To your soul He will reveal the precious essence
of this secret.

He, The Exalted Lord God

Through the four elements —
water, wind, earth and fire —

And on the axis of Four, Five,
Seven, Nine, and Six,

Behold existence's manifestations,
and more magnificent yet,

Should the one revelation illumine your heart,
then keep the vow of silence dear.

Chanteh—Realm of the Sufi
Molana Shah Maghsoud Sadegh Angha
"Pir Oveyssi"

He, The Exalted Lord God

That fire that sparks the pendulum of time and
bestows life to the soul,

That divine inspiration of Sadegh —
that savored essence of all spirits,

That water of life, that wavy munificence
imaged into form by the eyes,

What happened to That?
What became of It?

That witness of the glorious awarenesses as infinite as the witnessed,

That seer of feverish hearts in the select body and the world,

That worshipper of tenderness —
that Deity's imparting breath of life,

That lover's kindled heart, absorbed by the Beloved's compelling lure,

That reflector of light through the prism's wall,

That great assembly — that predicted promise,

That extender of relief to the
earth-leavened shell and its loads,

That eddy of folded powers, concealed within
the preserved tablet,

That safeguarded fervent ecstasy —
that absorbs and revives,

That radiant magnificent star, as a shooting star
that descends and penetrates,

That pure distilled frenzy of love —
that creator of Names,

What happened to That?
What became of It?

*That ebullient burgeoning within the structure
of particles,*

*That bed of ruffled hair imprinted with the tender
breeze of the pure,*

*That murmur of ever-expanding waves
and heavens,*

*That morning hubbub of the early riser, arousing
hundred clamours in existence's dome,*

*That incendiary sigh that harvests with fire a
hundred enraptured suns of love's frenzy,*

*That silent fermenting of the vein of vine surging
through with drunkenness,*

That pure effulgence that sets to glow the alum and the glass,

That mirror-like treasury of secrets undivulged — the stable and the bestower,

That nurtured intoxication beheld in the cup-bearer's cup,

That reviving wave, resurging from the breeze of dawn,

That beam of justice soaring to the heavens most high,

What happened to That?
What became of It?

*That child-like joyfulness, the fervor which
nourishes the inner self,*

*That vernal showering rain and that lustrous
gleaming pearl,*

*That enshrined beauty wending through the
mountainous skirts,*

*That fount of the sun hidden behind the darkness of
a hundred veils,*

That quivering and glittering dew of life,

*That water drop, flowering to bloom the
gardens of paradise,*

That rejoicing bud, the nightingale's heart,

That lily, that hyacinth, that tulip and the foliage,

*That blood-straining spring in the fields of
endearing madness,*

That burnt branded heart within the tulip's bloom,

*That submission of the submitted that became
wings for the heavens,*

**What happened to That?
What became of It?**

That trust which is the honor of virtuous souls

That entrusted jewel, waywardly circling the unknowns,

See how it's flaunted on desires of dust and earth,

Realities became despairing slaves covered by their earthenware,

Beds of carcass became the purpose for the powers and strengths,

In this cesspool the kite snapped away the lily's scent,

*Weakness fueled misfortune's strength of mud
as a mirage,*

*The flower's throne submerged into the
swampland of layers — dead,*

*Strengths into impotence turned and tenderness
into earthly molds consumed,*

*In disappointment of the children of greed,
slaves to the earth,*

*A thousand sighs of Adam ascended to the dome
of existence,*

**What happened to That?
What became of It?**

How can I not divulge, this was the treasure
that was interred.

✧ ✧ ✧

O soul of souls, my soul wasn't all you
took away,

My heart and belief you pillaged as well.

Your alluring and shining guidance kindles,

The flaming dance of passion and ecstasy so dear.

My share from your everlasting and
inspiring soul I take,

'Til absolute awareness is my enraptured state.

Though, I'm enclosed in the coercion of time,

Yet, the resplendent flame of this lantern I am.

Unfold my wings, set me to fly,

From the fortress of these dungeon walls,
my liberation grant.

Written on the birthday of the lord of the saints,
the king of truth, Ali Morteza (peace be upon him)

Wednesday
13 Rajab 1408
12 Esfand 1366
2 March 1988

The *Secret Word*

Introduction

*I*n a previous publication of divine poetic thought, *Message from the Soul*, the author's father, Molana Shah Maghsoud Sadegh Angha, centers his inspired chant upon a recurring phrase: "the source of life in the heart." This is our key to the comprehension of *The Secret Word*, a narrative poem that springs not from the brain, with its questionable energy, but purely, simply, from the heart. This prayer-poem, remarkably takes on rhythm, musicality, form, meaning, and lyricism equal to many of our great works of written art. It is a testament to the truth that the heart knows all things and can, in fact, render them into language in exquisite detail and emotion. We can believe the work was written to demonstrate this principle.

I was fortunate enough to interview Molana Salaheddin Ali Nader Shah Angha, the leader of Maktab Tarighat Oveyssi Shahmaghsoudi *(School of Islamic Sufism)*, about his writing of *The Secret Word*. I was not surprised to be told that the words had visited this master through the night and that he wrote the language as it moved through him. As one reads the work, it becomes amazingly clear that this is not the writing of formulation and form, but of a sense far deeper — a vibration one receives but cannot demand or will.

The epigraph, "Our share of everything granted through eternity, through our efforts cannot be greatened one bit," is a prophesy of the unfolding of the poem, for it not only suggests the tenor of the text as we begin but also describes the process by which it was written. "Efforts" is the key word here, for this is not the sort of poem that could be brought to life through effort. It is the form of writing that is divinely inspired.

As entry to the poem, a premise emerges within the first line: "Ever arising Love grants life." Simple, concrete words, as simple and concrete as the sun or the stars. We could go a long way in literature without encountering such a crystalline statement of purpose. Each subsequent line on the first page, we find, is a line unto itself with its own mysteries, messages, and verbal translucence. As a student of literature and a writer of poetry, I moved slowly through the intensity of the lines in wonder and fear of what I would find. I had embarked upon a reading to consider this poem's place among other poems now being translated to English. Would I perceive the object on the page in its quickening as poetry, poetry as I know it from a Western perspective? Surely, no one of us expects to read words that really teach us the secret of existence. How can we be led to a vision that is not ours? And how do we confront another's explanation of the divine without confusion? The fear encountered is only that we will not be included in the divine dream. Quietly, without rhetoric or preachment, the words seem to embrace us, words which in themselves could be empty but which instead focus upon a kind of energy and motion. The motion comes from the poet's evocation of belief within each line, and the spiraling of a central image which conveys the signification through to a statement of belief. Because of the unconscious choice of words, magical and light, there is a continuum and flow — words turned to sound.

Is it poetry or a highly rarified prayerform? Is it a blessing? An unveiling of thought learned throughout centuries of devotion? What is the essence found here? How do I apply standards of poetic practices to a work so impossible to categorize and impossible to contain? Usually I can only understand what I read by understanding the drama found in the act of the imagination, but most certainly the human imagination is not at work here. In *The Secret Word*, the author as prophet is still a man who is writing a poem. This draws us in. This poem, however, was given to its author as a vehicle for "seeing" the reality of truth. Revelation is at work here.

This particular author we are reading is not only a poet but also a physicist, scientist, mathematician, and spiritual master. The multiple intelligences are evidenced in the use of material images from the earth and nature mingled and mixed with perceptions of reality. Philosophical thought, yes; visions of truth, yes. Now I am at home with the work.

The idea of poem as revelation is a long standing one in English literature. Its value exists within the complexity of the revelation so that the poetic line transcends the finite thought form. We can see this at work in *The Secret Word*. The speaker provides kernals of revelatory language that place us within a kind of understanding based on hope. The voyage of the poem proposes a call to faith, but it also constructs a world of perception beyond the physical world yet in the service of the physical world. Although the central identification of the author is to God, the poem is always the expression of a mortal man describing the substance of being alive on this earth. We have the experience of the reality of religion in poetic form. We have a concept poem of redemption that does not use cultural history to tell its story, does not refer to moments of observation, but instead brings us to a condition of awakening through enigma made available with simple powerful language. We are shown in *The Secret Word* sensations of the inner voice in a journey of the soul. They are words describing the truth and not philosophical hypotheses. The words have a multidimensional character, providing a new scope for the reader to view each dimension of creation as a unified system.

We have writing here which demonstrates with modesty and dignity the experience of self/God-realization and invites us to share this:

Formed Essence,
Self-Evident Words,
Sun, the Protector,
The Worshipping Moon,
The Prostrating Stars,
Equilibrium, the sky,
Human from clay,
Two Green Leaves,
Receptions and diffusion: Divine dispensation,
And the eternal melody hums of Existence,
The heavenly kingdom speaks of His Oneness . . . .

The Secret Word is a meditation for those who believe and practice Sufi mysticism. It is also a poem that can satisfy others who love and appreciate a vision beautifully told.

Grace Cavalieri
February 4, 1988
Washington, D.C.

The Secret Word

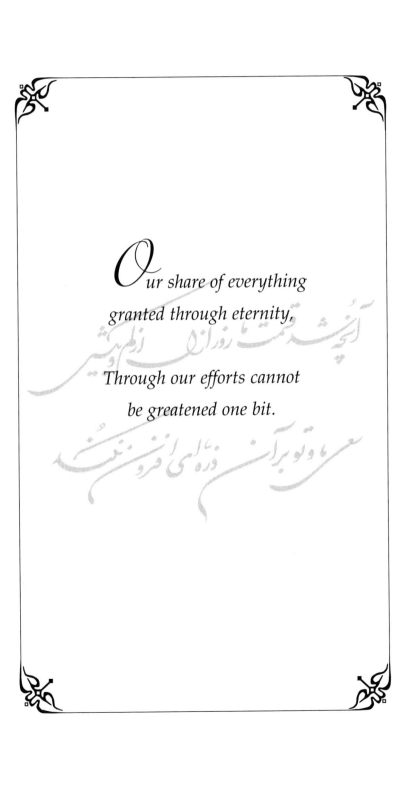

*O*ur share of everything
granted through eternity,

Through our efforts cannot
be greatened one bit.

He, the Exalted Lord God

Ever arising Love grants life,

Movement from life ensues and water transmits,

The particle settled on the node and the node upon circles revolves,

Circles are waves and waves are forever expanding,

Water, vapor, dust, and clay mingled,

And in the glow of Love's translucent fire images form,

And tranquillity is firm,

Membranes persistently generate the veils,

And veils preserve the light,

The realm of spirits is the delicate aspect of bodies,

And the delicate bodies are the knowledgeable agents of the corpse,

Has feet but walks not, has hands but takes not,

Eyes and ears exist but neither see nor hear,

Immersed and confounded in darkness,

Appended to the placenta,

Waiting without desire, without wish,

The tree of cogitation bears no fruit,

It is dependent but separate,

*Equilibrium and resurrection speak for the forces
and sources, based upon predestination,*

It is the exact and the peak of love and oneness,

Nurtures and accepts without interference,

Goodness is the seed of truth and purity,

Innately submitted, healthy and sincere,

Initiator and initiated,

Cause and effect,

Appears in darkness and has no need to know,

Unaware of its greatness,

On the way, yet unaware,

Has no opinion of birth,

Has no concept of time,

Devoid of space and place,

Encompassed in solitude and silence,

A captive without desire for freedom,

It is the Word itself and not a discourse,

Eloquent for the truth of self,

It is absolute movement from movement
by movement,

The intelligence of the atom is the exact knowledge,

Born in birth,

And in tranquility it is the Celestial Divinity,

By Divine grace dispersion converges into
concentration,

And the concentrated into unity evolves,

A point expanded and diffused,

Internally from every direction it became a motion,

Every fiber was thus touched and impressed,

The moment of deliverance is at hand,

Time to leave the contracted chamber,

Without hesitation, without hurry,

In spiral crest and fall,

From the source of water to clay,

From the contracted chamber released to the spacious realm,

All windows are cast open,

And the bent back from its heavy load released,

Freed unto a wave of light,

❖❖❖

Life grants life and Love is the guardian of life,

The lonely leaves the placenta,

And breaks all chains.

The cry of "I" echoes in existence,

The canticles of angels greet the newborn,

And the newborn, stable in tranquility, is
spectacular and overwhelming,

Shadows are the manifestation of the moving images
of movement,

And movement is saturated,

And light is the interpretation of shadows,

Windows open to reflecting shadows are the porters of news,

And reflections and vibrations assail and storm the senses,

Silence is shattered, uproar ensues,

And streams of information self-generating and unfamiliar,

Nature is deceived by the mantle of nature,

Opportunists disrupt the tranquility,

Falling from one trap into another,

Slave of shadows sees and hears,

Attachments are caused in fear of shadows,

And need is the connecting link to the outside world,

The child of light departs for the land of shadows,

True knowledge is replaced by acquisitions,

Turbulences demolish the house,

Desires dominate,

And the master becomes the servant and the slave,

Natural appetite, is insatiable,

And greed is nothing but enslavement,

Pursuit of desire is obstinance in ignorance,

Imprisoned to the mass of indigents,

Learns crooked ways,

In bondage the slave became,

Wisdom by habit ruled,

And true knowledge is constrained by habitual consumption,

Base relationships human purity despoil,

The pure takes the cloak of dust,

The high-flying bird of the skies into vulture turns,

The delicate is subsumed by harshness,

Alone, became lonelier,

And the true self is lost,

Darkness, ignorance, and corruption cast their
shadows,

And the window of hope is obstructed,

And a heavy lock bars the door,

Demons, cellular instigations,

Gates of desire, the fire-temple of insatiable envy,

And the offspring of greed, anger, envy, and passions.

And Cain, Abel smothers in the womb of earth,

The Divine Treasure is unseen in the pursuit of impurities,

In illness befuddled by joy,

And in loss proudly reaping profits,

Alas, evil and ugliness are firmly rooted,

And the agents of corruption and destruction,

Lies in place of truth,

Ugliness in place of beauty

Evil in place of kindness have enthroned,

And a mirage is taken for the Water of Life,

Outward attractions conceal the reality,

And the alluring masks of illusion prompt the
intelligence to fabricate the outer world,

Ambitious in repairing the ancient ruin,

And life in a bubble has become the explanation for
Life,

Definitions by the senses do not speak of life's true
essence.

Death's bell counts the seconds,

And time is the cradle of oblivion,

Death of shadows awakens not the ignorant,

Ears hear but have no audition,

Eyes see but have no vision,

There are no infinite results in limited experiences.

Imaginary mirages are the shroud for the self-taught,

And intelligence had no effective point.

Fire destroys the harvest,

And desire is the breath of destruction,

The miscarried fetus has no one to turn to,

The lost are preys of desire and move along the wrong path of life,

He who knows true life fears not death,

One nourishing in the womb has no knowledge of the sustainer,

And the ignorant acknowledge not the learned.

Birth is the moment of death, and death is the ascent of the delicate,

Vibrations are the secondary hearth of life,

Whatever is seen outwardly and imagined inwardly is illusion,

Whatever is witnessed through the heart and observed externally is truth,

Thought is a fluctuating bridle,

And will is superior to thought.

The force of desire makes everything promiscuous.

Equilibrium of absorptions is the point of freedom.

Independence from bonds,

*And patience in equilibrium is the stability
of the virtuous,*

The basis of morality is free will,

*And faith and love are based on uniformity
of the true will,*

And love is the foundation of virtue.

Tulips dance to the breeze in the tulip garden.

And the warbler songs of the love of Existence,

The impurities burn,

The receptor of Knowledge is freed.

The Son of Man[1] is viewed in Man,

*The acquainted each other seek and strangers each
other meet,*

And lover of the Beloved is the lover,

True wishes are unconditional.

Poisoned arrows sought no target.

And guidance is the bed-rock of freedom,

Outer calmness is the reflection of inner awareness,

*And the exterior world is the broken image of
the inner senses,*

Hope is planted seed in fertile ground that bears fruit.

*In the land of my heart the plant of despair
never grows.*

The cry of the silent by the flame of love ascends,

*And the heavens listen to the heart-wishes of
the sincere,*

O Thou, Lord of the Arif's[2] heart,

For the bestowment of the great care of the Masters,

For the strength of heart of the youthful ones,

For the enraptured love-call of awakened hearts,

For the holiness and purity of the attestors of Truth,

And for the heavenly innocence of Tulip-Growers,[3]

Enflame my essence with Thy flame of Love,

For the Love of Sadegh's Dawn,[4]

For the Glorified Sun of Gratitude, Ahmad,[5]

And for the majesty and dignity of the
Glorious One,[6]

By the glorious illuminations of the Almighty,

For the Forty Guiding Lanterns of Sufism,[7]

Guide the Child of Fate to the Predestined Goal.[8]

And remove the leaves of death from the branches of life,

And by the truth of Divine and everlasting Knowledge,

By the truth of the awareness in the elevated Mountain of Ghaf,[9]

Clear the dust of shadows from the illumined face,

And reveal the identity.

Time has arrived,

The talisman and boundaries of time are broken,

Place is interlaced,

An unlimited tremor demolished the boundaries,

All things from every direction became united,

*And the endless heavens are adorned by the dawn of
Truth,*

And the ancient song by Venus was played.

*Through the vastness of the heavens there was
nothing but the truth,*

Neither Eastern nor Western,

And at the summit of the skies,

And at the cleavage of the horizons,

And the Crescent of Oneness,

The Father's call summons the child.

And the hearts of heavenly angels are instilled with hope and tranquility,

And the shore of salvation is in sight,

Darkness is demolished,

And the brilliance of the spoken light conquers all,

The heavenly melodies of Love caress the listener.

The splendor of spring blossoms,

Unfolded on the tree of life,

Our palm tree of hope became fruitful,

With Languishing Fragrance,[10]

And dew drops glittering upon the fruit of hope,

And the eternal promise of everlasting life,

Glowed from shores to shore,

Life saved its child from the river of blood,

The melody in the Seven Domes became the Eternal Essence of speech,

O Thou who Thy promise kept,

O Thou residing in the Golden Fortress,

O Thou unchangeable in the Glorious Almighty,

Thou art the Munificent, for all in the world of prevalence,

Absolute Merciful,

Expanded Laws,

Formed Essence,

Self-Evident Words,

Sun, the Protector,

The Worshipping Moon,

The Prostrating Stars,

Equilibrium, the Sky,

Human from Clay,

Two Green Leaves,

Receptions and diffusion: Divine Dispensation,

And the Eternal melody hums of Existence,

The heavenly kingdom speaks of His Oneness,

And creation is imbued with His penetrating breath,

The day indicates the manifestations,

And the night signifies cognition and knowledge,

The colorless is concealed in colors,

And stability is self-existent in equilibrium,

Rays are from the sun,

And the firmament revolves by His Commandments.

Existence is self-evident to His words,

Sadegh speaks through Nader,[11]

The body of light dissolves in Light,

The drop to the sea returns,

The Sun engulfs the skies,

Thus, when he became stable, I imbued him with My Spirit.

The tranquility of the true human heart is glorious,

Life emerges only from life,

No-thing can be other than what it is.

Whatever is, always has been and will be forever.

There can be but One Eternal,

Not arising from anything and unchangeable,

Because of the oneness in appearance and essence, it must be stable.

Existence arises in the existent without doubt.

As a sheathed sword is the Almighty God.

All is annihilated,

Eternity is the Face of God,

He is the Sun of the Heavenly Divine,[12]

The firmaments are clearsighted by His light,

Mohammad's Love[13] *is glorious,*

He is the Love of lovers,

Light is Self-Perceptible,

He is Self-Evident in the earth and skies,

Refracted Light in diamond, He is,

Mount Sinai's kindling fire, He is,

He giveth wisdom unto whom He wills,

Allah is the Omnipotent.

Everything will perish but His Face,

Thus, seek the path leading to Allah.

O Lord, for the sake of the pure awakened hearts,

In remembrance of those blessed by Thy Grace,

For the sake of their sincerity and love,

For the sake of the joyous call of the risers at dawn,

Let saints of Heart accept my Book,

Sing out my Love, declare my Call of Love.

Aban 26, 1363
Safar 23, 1405
November 17, 1984

Glossary

of Selected Names and Terms

1. *Man* — The true human essence that is not subject to male or female gender classifications. It refers to Adam which is equivalent to the word "being."

2. *Arif* — The one who has attained the most exalted state of existence through annihilation in the Almighty God.

3. *Tulip Growers* — The Elect who guide the seeker of Truth.

4. *Sadegh's Dawn* — Molana Shah Maghsoud Sadegh Angha, the forty-first Holy Teacher of Maktab Tarighat Oveyssi Shahmaghsoudi *(School of Islamic Sufism)*.

5. *Glorified Sun of Gratitude, Ahmad* — Molana Mir Ghotbeddin Moham-mad Angha, the fortieth Holy Teacher of Maktab Tarighat Oveyssi Shahmaghsoudi *(School of Islamic Sufism)*.

6. *Glorious One* — Molana Jalaleddin Ali Mir Abolfazl Angha, the thirty-ninth Holy Teacher of Maktab Tarighat Oveyssi Shahmaghsoudi *(School of Islamic Sufism)*.

7. *Forty Guiding Lanterns of Sufism* — The Holy Teachers of Maktab Tarighat Oveyssi Shahmaghsoudi *(School of Islamic Sufism)*.

8. *Predestined Goal* — Molana Salaheddin Ali Nader Shah Angha, the forty-second Holy teacher of Maktab Tarighat Oveyssi Shahmaghsoudi *(School of Islamic Sufism)*.

9. *Elevated Mountain of Ghaf* — The Almighty's Dominion.

10. *Languishing Fragrance* — *Divan Masnavi Ravayeh*, by Molana Salaheddin Ali Nader Shah Angha.

11. *Sadegh* — Molana Shah Maghsoud Sadegh Angha.
Nader — Molana Salaheddin Ali Nader Shah Angha.

12. *Sun of the Heavenly Divine* — His Holy Eminence, Amir-al Mo'menin Ali (peace be upon him), the first Imam of the Shi'a.

13. *Mohammad's Love* — The Holy Prophet of Islam, Hazrat Rassoul Akram (peace and blessings upon him).

Prophet Mohammad
Imam Ali

Hazrat Oveys Gharani*
Hazrat Salman Farsi
Hazrat Habib-ibn Salim Ra'i
Hazrat Soltan Ebrahim Adham
Hazrat Abu Ali Shaqiq al-Balkhi
Hazrat Sheikh Abu Torab Nakhshabi
Hazrat Sheikh Abi Amr al-Istakhri
Hazrat Abu Ja'far Hazza
Hazrat Sheikh Kabir Abu Abdollah Mohammad-ibn Khafif Shirazi
Hazrat Sheikh Hossein Akkar
Hazrat Sheikh Morshed Abu-Isshaq Shahriar Kazerouni
Hazrat Khatib Abolfath Abdolkarim
Hazrat Ali-ibn Hassan Basri
Hazrat Serajeddin Abolfath Mahmoud-ibn Mahmoudi Sabouni Beyzavi
Hazrat Sheikh Abu Abdollah Rouzbehan Baghli Shirazi
Hazrat Sheikh Najmeddin Tamat-al Kobra Khivaghi
Hazrat Sheikh Ali Lala Ghaznavi
Hazrat Sheikh Ahmad Zaker Jowzeghani
Hazrat Noureddin Abdolrahman Esfarayeni
Hazrat Sheikh Alaoddowleh Semnani
Hazrat Mahmoud Mazdaghani
Hazrat Amir Seyyed Ali Hamedani
Hazrat Sheikh Ahmad Khatlani
Hazrat Seyyed Mohammad Abdollah Ghatifi al-Hasavi Nourbakhsh
Hazrat Shah Ghassem Feyzbakhsh
Hazrat Hossein Abarghoui Janbakhsh
Hazrat Darvish Malek Ali Joveyni
Hazrat Darvish Ali Sodeyri
Hazrat Darvish Kamaleddin Sodeyri
Hazrat Darvish Mohammad Mozaheb Karandehi (Pir Palandouz)
Hazrat Mir Mohammad Mo'men Sodeyri Sabzevari
Hazrat Mir Mohammad Taghi Shahi Mashhadi
Hazrat Mir Mozaffar Ali
Hazrat Mir Mohammad Ali
Hazrat Seyyed Shamseddin Mohammad
Hazrat Seyyed Abdolvahab Naini
Hazrat Haj Mohammad Hassan Kouzekanani
Hazrat Agha Abdolghader Jahromi
Hazrat Jalaleddin Ali Mir Abolfazl Angha
Hazrat Mir Ghotbeddin Mohammad Angha
Hazrat Molana Shah Maghsoud Sadegh Angha
Hazrat Salaheddin Ali Nader Shah Angha

The conventional Arabic transliteration is Uwais al-Qarani

Genealogy of Maktab Tarighat Oveyssi Shahmaghsoudi
(School of Islamic Sufism)